A Shared Life

Winner of the Edwin Ford Piper Poetry Award

Publication of this book was made possible

with the generous assistance of Janet Piper

A Shared Life

POEMS BY

Katherine Soniat

University of Iowa Press Ψ Iowa City

University of Iowa Press,

Iowa City 52242

Copyright © 1993 by

Katherine Soniat

All rights reserved

Printed in the United States

of America

Design by Richard Hendel

Printed on acid-free paper

Library of Congress Cataloging-in-

Publication Data

Soniat, Katherine.

  A shared life: poems / by Katherine

Soniat.

      p.   cm.—(Edwin Ford Piper

poetry award)

    ISBN 0-87745-429-9 (pbk.)

    I. Title.   II. Series.   III. Series:

Iowa poetry prize.

PS3569.O65396S53   1993

811′.54—dc20   93-13695

                                              CIP

97 96 95 94 93 P 5 4 3 2

For Rick, and for Catawba

Since the wild animal's back now is your shoulder,

And since the miracle of not-being is finished,

Start then, poet, a song at the edge of it all

To death, to silence, and to what does not return.

—Antônio Machado

Contents

Acknowledgments

Many thanks to the editors of the following journals
in which these poems first appeared.

American Scholar: "Gifts"

American Voice: "Mount View
Pure"

*Anthology of the University of
Southern California*: "Deer
Season Again"

Antioch Review: "What We
Keep"

Artemis: "Taking Possession"

*Breadloaf Anthology of Nature
Poetry*: "A Shared Life,"
"October Bestiary"

Devil's Millhopper: "Janus in
Autumn," "Telling Time"

First Things: "In a Dark
Country Night"

Greensboro Review: "Think
about It," "Terrestrial"

Iowa Review: "Marks of Light,"
"The Springhouse"

Kenyon Review: "Distance and
Design"

Laurel Review: "Prediction"
(entitled "Lightning Rods")

Literary Review: "Crivelli's
Pietà Angel"

Nation: "A Comparable Season"

New England Review: "In Spite
of Forgetting"

New Laurel Review: "Desire"

New Orleans Review: "The
Next Day," "Balboa in
Spring"

New Virginia Review: "Story
Line," "Free-falling"

North Dakota Review: "From a
Vantage Point Overlooking
the Battle of Hanging Rock"

Ohio Review: "A Shared Life,"
"Fortune"

Outerbridge: "Other People's
Houses"

Plum Review: "A Short History
of Stray Bullets"

Poems for a Small Planet: "A
Shared Life," "October
Bestiary"

Poet Lore: "War"

Poetry: "Routing the Maps
Home" (entitled "Rose
Cloth"), "Right Here"
(entitled "Desire"), "Secrets
about Nothing," "Daughter,"
"Primary Motif"

Prairie Schooner: "Last Song," "Water Translation," "Making Ghosts," "Rhapsody," "Oranges and Rum at Noon"

Seneca Review: "The Future," "Bedside Story"

Shenandoah Review: "Two Daughters"

Southern Review: "Harboring"

Spoon River Poetry Review: "Full Grown," "Wanting It"

Tar River Poetry Review: "Some Vegetables and Stars"

Threepenny Review: "A Square in Mozambique"

Witness: "Graffiti," "October Bestiary," "Rings"

Yale Review: "Learning in Time"

Yankee: "Domestication"

Yarrow: "Primer"

Some of these poems first appeared in a chapbook, *Winter Toys*, published by the Green Tower Press, Maryville, Missouri.

Thanks to the Virginia Commission for the Arts for a generous grant which made this book possible.

Special thanks to Becky Cox for her help in the preparation of this manuscript.

One

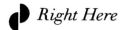 *Right Here*

At dark on Halloween
I pinch nasturtiums.
They snap like little fingers
on their way to being shadow.
Thinking of it, I see it's sad
what could happen. Or is it
sadder what's happening
in my hand: mist coating orange
wrinkles as another puzzle disappears,
our endings first too far,
then too close to understand?

And there is no help in space
as across two million light-years
we listen for the next galaxy,
while down deep the whale sings
for others twelve thousand miles away.
So we make the stars talk about us.
Tonight, the silent Pleiades shine
high in the Halloween sky. I picture
the rising, floating dead.

But dirt weights the fields
above the dead, and starlight holds
only the polish of what's gone.
That time I first looked
at you closely, you called it desire,
and I reached my hand out
into the thick of it.

 *The Future*

A city squared on the horizon
and smoke blowing from chimneys that jut
out of the wet, slate rooftops—
always this image arrives, seasonless,
from nowhere. Perhaps it was
that November, when alone at the window
I watched the afternoons mass themselves
like rain washing down a smoky day.

Or maybe this heat never was mine,
and memory got it backwards
in its own territorial way, insisting
it was me, of course, I was there—
when indeed it was sundown for some painter
needing warmth so much, he crossed
from the window and stroked it in,
turning it out as great clouds
of colored smoke I took as mine.

But what if this skyline never was
at all? This smoke could come to nothing
more than the tail end of need,
imagination drifting off into a future
that slips from the top of the sky down.

Fortune

Suppose the waiting began
with rain on a sleeping porch
while the tea leaves
                    darkened on a damask cloth.
The rose bed's pattern was one of petal rot,
singular, cold membranes
                    lifted from the backwash
of summer
        which goes

to say that now I know why
I can't shrug off October—
those days when everything hesitates
in the woods
                as if hearing a perfectly
                    timed clock strike
                        hollowly from its wooden case.

The impulse is toward silence, bird flight,
that roll of dots casting hush across the sky.

Once on a sleeping porch there was such a quiet,
along with the slow, late rain.
                        See
that small figure under the blue coverlet,
the child made from my own combination
of love and grief:
                    Now she's starting
                    to breathe in
what later the roses will set off.

The past is beginning
                    its oblique sift down—
a random parade of all
she'll not quite remember.

Look
        at her eyelids.
        She's stopped by some initial confusion.
Perhaps it's the makings of a mother
                            or of a far-off
marriage that make her flicker
as the silvery combination
                        of her future turns
                        and clicks,
                        turns and ticks,
her eyes recording the countless, small shocks.

Domestication

Two stories up on the screen porch
where the blue parakeet swung to the rain,
clucking past twilight at her barred cage,

I lay in my fabric house of sheets,
a lamp, and overstuffed chairs—
their corduroy backs offering something

solid under the white cotton sky.
The rain trickled down outside the porch,
beyond this assembly of linens

slung close to the lamplight, a moon
wrapped in cloth for my tropics.
Playing house was like praying with light,

asking a veiled shelter to hold steady,
bargaining with the green summer squall
to brighten and hush.

You and the moon taught silence.
In the boardinghouse, quiet
as a sleeping castle, you'd wake me
and hush me, and off we'd move
into the gardenia dark, headlights
and cigarettes in a snarl.
You must have been looking for someone
far away, someone you wanted
to come upon silently.

Other times you broke the silence,
waking me with a whisper to blow a good-bye
to mommy-kiss-over-the-moon.
You pointed to the moon, then slipped
away. Stayed away and came back.
I grew seasick with your dissolve,
your arrangement as something

remembered—your hands went out
to me as if to say come down to the shore,
be part of the drift, the mother-daughter
pairs speckling the brilliant dunes.
I reached out and you shifted
into gardenias, perfume rounding
the corner, a bruise slipped
over the moon.

My stepfather-to-be parked
under an oak near the streetcar stop
and pointed to the dashboard clock
after delivering my mother
to her two o'clock plane.

I was five and knew time only
as the clink of silvery triangles
in my kindergarten rhythm band,
or as the number of maroon cars
that my mother and I counted

before Mrs. Murphy's eight o'clock
car pool came crunching through the acorns.
Morning was a counting game:
one, two, three maroon cars,
the streetcar accenting each

with a clang, before the firm honk
of Mrs. Murphy. But today
this new man and I had come
to a halt. He wanted a fatherly deed
and said to watch how the hands move

clockwise, always to the right,
the big one methodical as a stick
tapping the blackboard dark,
the smaller hand following,
the smallest one almost frantic

to get ahead, be on time.
In the front seat, afternoon spread
out as the minutes and days
my mother would be gone. I wanted
to count backwards to the quiet space

before her plane flew away. But
I was told to catch on, and finally,
my lesson learned, we pulled up
near the streetcar on its iron track,
the gears shifting from first, to second,

then third. I felt us jerk ahead.

Oranges and Rum at Noon

A radio's violins slip through the air
like heat loose in the palmettoes,
the Seagrove Market leaning wooden and sandy
as thirty years ago—
its corner phone still the one phone,
sun deepening the gulf to that old
clear green.
       And maybe you are up the road
again, behind the door we slammed on each other
after two weeks too much vacation at thirteen.
Azalea Street curves on the bluff above the sea,
and that man and woman from the summer cottage
seem in this salt air too:
            oranges, rum
on the porch at noon, and the inland lake
swimming on their bare skins all afternoon—
and you and I taken in,
          imagining it easy
for lives to glisten like that.

—for Pierce

Balboa in Spring

These are the flashing green days
when clouds rush with March,

and the man over the back fence
shouts happily in Spanish
like Balboa on his peak.

He breathes the same air
the flowering fields tilt in.

It's summed up by the sleepy dog
rolling in the sun, measuring
out his lazy whine

over the new spring mint,
motioning *yes*
in all but Spanish.

As we drive the misted mountain road,
looking down on a valley mounting its own
argument, all the damp spring young
wobbling up from the ground, you turn
to me and suggest a child.

Do you want this even as things suggest
themselves, then disappear?
Gravity's a dangerous field for twos,
and the stars have dwarf doubles
that devour. They glitter above
our swelling lot.

Do I want this because of what's lacking,
or because time's a summer marsh humming
with what is? The mist is single-minded
as the stars. Absence is what we see.
And you are beside me, looking.

◗ Story Line

Once a story came in a dream
and every answer seemed
incomplete.

What's the moon for?
That was the question, and your voice
answered clearly *it's a boundary*

to wait inside. I said *yes*
but was seeing the moon spill out
as those shadowy arrangements

we learn and relearn by,
and already you were changing
the words, shaping the question

into my answer: *You don't know.*
Do you ever know what you want?
I nodded,

thinking *no*
as you went on explaining
me to me like that.

Water Translation

Today it's a dusty sun
and I think of rain on my thighs,
cold liquid in my mouth.

               The corn rows are
wasting away in this dry noon of gnats.

I feel it and say

       oranges

            to the blue field heat.
I tell you that one summer, all summer,
I rolled that waxy fruit

          in my palms,
pushing a long straw down deep.
I squeezed and sucked up the opening globes of juice
and at night

       the salt marsh sounded with
       breed,

         breed.

          Everything repeated.
In the enamel basin brimming with rain
under the oak, larvae swam—

           those hatching young
        scribbling into shapes of life.
All of us loose in a summer of rainwater.

Such poignancy vanished in the corn heat.
I cross the doorsill

       for shade,
       wind the clock,

each tick setting aside the moist
familiarity of offspring.
                        I've tried
to give you the scent, and you ask why
I look at you
                  like this.

Desire

An April bear
plunges spray from the watercress stream—
hunger, the first awakening of any.

His yellow teeth open, flash with it,
and the seasons pass away.

                Finally,
it was all like being hungry,
and afterwards, the winter sleep.

Two

The hornets enter this dark
nest filled with one great hum.
It's hard to think of each
with will enough to hang the earth
from an Appalachian power line—
and something has plugged one golden
ear of corn above the entrance hole,
thrust it into the practical mud
daubed up, then down, the curve
of every invitation
and departure.
          In late October
the landscape assumes a wrinkled look.
Is it just exhaustion, that sleepy
hornet hum? It makes me picture chilled
migrants, and the hornets stay close
as if some door kept thudding,
reminding each of home.
                When the first
freeze empties the black hallway
and a season, their gray,
waved efforts remain.

Gifts

Driving past the river cemetery,
he pointed to a shade patch
near the shoreline, saying
that's where he'd be buried,
and it struck me that for forty
years I had not known his birth date.

He gave me a gift that day—
his watercolor painting of hats
in the hall closet: the elegant
black top hat which is
out of magic, the gray herringbone
cap woven for stone villages

by the sea. Old hats, older hats, generations
of hats tipped in respect, soon to be closeted
away. Back home, I set out to find
him a first and perfect birthday gift,
and found him as the father I barely
knew—each birthday card too personal

and sly about the paradox of years,
each gift perhaps too effeminate, like the blue
lap blanket I gave him last Christmas.
He exchanged it for a green hunting shirt.
None of us wants to be taken
for what's left in the mirror.

Then I spotted the khaki cap
in the store window on Main, and I could
almost glimpse the two of us under the same
hat, my mother saying again, *you're his*
spit, that's how much you look like him.
I thought of our first exchange.

Making Ghosts

At first glance, it seems
a glorification squeezed through the hand—
man and all the animals
given a home in space;

man discovering how to speak
of his dead in present tense
as if they could come in out of the rain,
their ghosts cloudy and distant.

Until one day, juicy in the sunlight,
lives start falling down,
keep falling down, and it's one of us
gathering our own

into the milk blue vases, fearful.
The years arrive from out of nowhere
when a shelf slides forth,
metallic, with one face

shining back. We back
away. The animals too must hear
the snap in the brush.
They spark to it like flint,

making a bristle and hiss of themselves,
man's old companions
breathing hard,
cornered in space.

In a Dark Country Night

I see one bumblebee heading
over the fence and into the doorway
of this shrunken Old Field's Baptist Church.
The trees are tagged with signs
of modern advancement: KEEP OUT,
BAD DOGS, as out of the big house
comes a white-haired man saying
he's Harry Smith, maker of this
miniature, and everything is copacetic
if I want to take a look.
Just be sure to keep *him*
in my story.

The real church has vanished
from the hill, but here's a six-foot-long
god-house that Harry Smith built
in his living room before turning it
out to winter.

The steeple strung with Christmas lights
soars in Wonderland proportions
over the roof's peeling coat of red
as I stoop for the peep show,
overturned four-inch pews scatter
chance into a sanctuary;
wasps with wafer-thin wings
fly before cellophaned windows,
the altar lit in a dusky, underwater blue.

No parishioners puzzle in a stain
of sunlight. This church
is cleansed of people,
of all but the ceremony of cutting,
the ritual of nailing
disappearance into place.

That night the big church came down,
it must have spread its cloistered parts
like stars in a dark country night
till Harry took charge and planted
in his yard what anyone will remember
of Old Field's Baptist Church.

I'm on my knees
and he's still saying *remember me*,
holding out his photo
of the first, the big and the real
one. So, in the language of installation,
I commit Harry and his church,
hatched in a house, to shine
as blue as bedside stars over Old Field's.
A far clock chimes in midsummer.
It's midday.

◖ *Last Song*

Two weeks of rot and the blacksnake
bleaches down to vertebrae

scattered like crumbs of jasmine
on the asphalt. Blacksnake,

bad snake, redistributed to Kingdom Come
when once it was the symbol

for life's unending circle——a solution
to the earthworm's reconnoitering

for two lives out of every one;
a rejoinder to the snail's hunched glimmer

as it travels to the edge of this
world-without-end, its knobbed horns

nodding like fools' caps: O, sing
the song of fools, rasping

of armory and shells, the screech
of hard right angles out of sync

with snakes and snails slipping
like lubricants through time.

Mount View Pure

On a blank page in the Gideon Bible
I began this poem, hearing whistling

trains and one everlasting dog
baying for a little more moon

in his dirt yard. This was where the hills
had let me down again and flattened out

into the deep South—the new South
where that evening I almost left

the road upon seeing a herd of southern
buffalo mixing it up with the droll cows,

car radio bleating with the voice of a writer,
carefully noting his chief influence

as Bugs Bunny. And there I was, headed home
again, approaching the El Ranchero Motor Court

OWNED AND OPERATED BY 100% AMERICANS.
I followed another sign to yet another

cheap room—the Mount View's night office,
thick with cardamon and curry, the Indian

woman saying *sign here* on a counter cluttered
with every good plastic saint and its cousins.

Next morning, out for a run,
I ran into a view of the county dump

and on past the collection box
marked FOR BULLIED CHILDREN AND WIVES

CALL 344 FOR QUICK PICK UP. Down the gravel
road, an old man leaned from his porch swing

to note that this was an exclusive neighborhood—
his house alone in the hot, green loblollies;

a rusted sign declaring BRIDGE WASHOUT;
the creek, a tumble of concrete

and lavishly flowering weed.

Her silences held like a season
of snow,
              never *hush* or *sit here.*
Just her hand rising to the window
in a fist, the two small girls
staring by her elbow.

Her hand,
              paused before the window that evening,
would remain like muscle in memory,
the girls' minds closing on

the emptiness
              of that foster home—
              she hardly believed in food,
              she didn't use words on them either.

But something was happening as she watched
the hired man disappear past the snow-drifted
barn, the loft hay.
              Going to town to tell,
he'd told the girls behind the barn. Now

the woman just seemed to know where he was
headed, her hand knotted before the pane,
her mouth whispering
              never.
The snow, thickening, almost made him
not there.

*

Our porch in May. The barn swallows' young
wait twenty-one days to dip from their nest,

fly, reeling with the simplicity of it,
hunger wanting to own its future

above an earth clustered with beetles.
They took off from the dirt-daubed

nest, and for days the swallow mates
believed in little birds that were

not there, pecking cats from the porch,
guarding twigs like a feathered past.

*

By August corn crackles with heat;
the poplars with locusts, their leaves
a torched orange, and the memory
of last year's flood is still so high,
the town grows giddy on disaster:
a secondhand bookstore thrusts up
a sign, AUTUMN IN CHERNOBYL IS WHEN THE BIRDS
CHANGE COLORS AND FALL FROM THE TREES.
They forget it's all of us kneeling
in this alarm of sun.

*

An old obsession, flight.
Imagine finding a way out—
holding ourselves glistening
high above the water, beyond
what's swirling at our feet.

Perhaps no different
than when whole regions toss
memory aside to glare at others
now a rock's throw away

while the future goes on
tensing, knotting at the window
like a fist. And swallows
circle an empty nest,
wrought with possibility.

Item

Lost: one 14K gold anklet worn about the neck
   of an eighteen-month-old last seen wandering
   in the Amoco station, wearing yellow
   designer jogging suit, British Knight
   tennis shoes. At midnight, he was
   circling the gas pumps like a dog
   remembering a leash. No one knew
   his name.

Found: the owner of the ankle bracelet, mother
   of the gas-pump baby, discovered the next day,
   a wad of bills in her fist, heaviness in her head.

Found: in a closet, a one-year-old, two-year-old, and
   a five-year-old; a family locked in
   so big brother could go out.

Found: in a bathroom at the Emergency Children's
   Facility, two four-year-olds having
   oral sex.

Unaccounted for: brother and sister dreaming
   on the urine-soaked mattress sleeping
   in the midst of broken sticks
   of furniture eight inches of clothes
   layering the floor the wood
   padded with dirt

Graffiti

With hearts and skulls and scarlet scrawls,
thousands swear at this boulder of a world

as if words could sting each passerby
into one sharp breath of recognition,

blame taken by the men in dark suits,
the fault resting with women

who ever wore red.

Learning in Time

I read of hospital hallways
crowded like wards,
of peasants, not soldiers, marooned
in a corridor's white light.
I learn the value of eyes
put out, how their dark will bleed
the State. But I am seeing
that hallway, its clock
where the one with his eyes
blown out is lifted by another
to relearn the face of a clock,
while somewhere off in a field
another is tugged from blasted corn
and left by a roadside mined for sheep
and those who tend the sheep.
This is the roadway that winds
to the white hallway where the hands
on one man hold the hands of another
to the hands of a clock.

A Square in Mozambique

These are the children
that no one went looking for.
It's as if each face here
had called out from the found-child
snapshots nailed up throughout the country,
saying to any aunt or uncle:
see some small part of your dead
brother or sister. Remember
me.

This is the village square
used for reunions of the lost,
where every look of recognition
is rewarded with a kit: clothes,
food, a hoe, and a bag of seed.
A dowry to grow human on,
or perhaps even to grow into the *clerk*
or *driver* that young Moneeka says
he wants one day to be.

Yesterday he kept saying that
as the plane ascended, flying him
away from his village where he no longer
was kin. He repeated himself
in the cool, drying air, thinking
he'd arrived at last in the chilled
garden of an aunt. But at night,
in the cinder-block receiving orphanage,
he fretted: what if no one came
to claim him at the morning display?

Morning comes in the square.
Men and women mill about, solemn-faced
even as their hand comes down
on a small child's shoulder
and eyes meet, saying *yes
it is you.* Here every face is dreamy
and hard, trying hard to remember.

Moneeka's aunt comes, fetches him.
She has remembered. At home
there is much to forget
but for the glass-paneled oven door
hung on the dirt wall—a frame
for her wedding photograph. Still,
she wants to see that day clearly.
She was clearly able to see Moneeka
as he peered from his found-child
photograph. In his face there was
her sister: his dead mother.

Over her hut the sun shifts
to the next day, and Moneeka's
batch of the lost-and-found
have been saved or put
in the orphanage to stay.
There is singing in the square,
and childish huddles squat
over games of rolling blue and green
marbles. Men unload fat sacks
of corn from a truck. No one thinks

to scramble after the spilt seed.
If a photograph were shot
one might forget—
with the singing faces,
the yellow corn and marbles in the dirt—
that this will never be
a game where the stakes are small.

A Comparable Season

The cedar waxwing has fallen
too much in love with the juniper berry
this rough winter, carried
his desire fermenting into spring.
We watch thawed skies fill with plunging
birds as cross country, the hunter,
sharp as daybreak, goes beyond his limit,
under the few remaining stars.

Three

Incinerator cans blaze
in back lots, crackle under the hands
of those who will not be found.
And insist on it. All the glistening
water filling an eye will not call
one back. No one even glances up
from a hand on the shoulder—
is that you?

*

Still we believe a benevolent surf
swells to wash things back.
At night, the wind suggests it,
curling shingles, billowing
screens, changing direction
in the bent trees.

*

Who was it that wandered out the screen door,
then disappeared? One moment, life was thick
as sighs on a night dizzy with mosquitoes.
Then, ivy darkened an empty room.
They said the phone rang for days.

*

Now, rain sheets before the mountains
and I want to route maps home,
over islands, the waters in between.
But, thinking back . . .
who left, you or me? You recall

how the trail ended, how abruptly.
I keep holding the shrubs away
over the last footprint
as clouds and sunlight scope the valley,
search for something gone.

*

Tonight, the moon's too heavy
and orange for the sky. I lie down
at dawn and guns go off in the hills,
rough sounds of things being laid out
in the frost: the doe who leaves
her ribs and face behind, the fox
ice-gauzed in his hushed, red fur.

*

In seconds breath falters
into the unheard-of. But
what can't be found, that's the sighing
part—rose cloth tattering from the barbed wire,
the footprint left by a country mailbox.
I would coax them back, wait
by the roadsides of the last-seen,
those patches of earth that become years,
one and two and three and

44

The Next Day

Today the sun's a simpler silver.
The field is cut,
the corn laid down.
Crows pick the earth
plucked to its finest pitch:
the day after,
when all is suddenly less.
Nothing can be forgotten.

Heat fogs from the parted
dirt. The sun presses
to the heart of a cloud.
What does not suggest itself?
Bulls breathe steam in the brook,
purple blossoms going under at their feet.

Deer Season Again

Before the window in the breezy feed shed,
deer mill about. Their brown bodies
shift back and forth,
and on the rusted oil drum a bobcat sits,
amber sunlight filtering down
like shades of river silt.
It is late afternoon in latest autumn,

but this twilight of animal-shadow
dwells where the stationary tilts,
and everything that moves is reborn
to the slippery and strange:
dream deer, bobcat, the shed starts

to slip downhill toward me. My dog
running off to meet it. For now
the deer browse the drifting floor.
The bobcat, perched sleepily, licks his paws
until the white tails flick once,
then twice, and there it is—a man
behind the oil drum, naked and greased
with gun in hand, antlers strapped to his head.
The bobcat bristles. Deer
freeze, and the dog rushes in to position himself
between the man and deer. Even as they move,
this arrangement holds—a carousel going round
with the faithfully fixed beasts.

From far away I am calling, whistling.
The shed stops its steady movement
to include me. The scene pauses at winter
in a lean-to, a man hunches
with fury in his skin. The only sound
is the clicking of a safety catch.
I am a passerby calling my animal away.

Taking Possession

We tool the infants' names in gold,
fit them with sailor suits,
and try to call them ours.

All navy blue and white
bathtubs brimful of clear water
under a brass-button sky—

Our policy is containment
as one by one the children spread,
grow, and we loom

expectant as ice shadows on the North Atlantic.

Crivelli's Pietà Angel

In life it was just another spring
plunging with trees and noon-dark weather.
Things went on from there,
betrayal aside.
But this angel's sopped eyes are beyond
consolation, stopped with a brokenness
the living feel about the dead.
And Crivelli must have known it,
with each gray, each plum daub to the sockets.

Somewhere this angel must have
a furious double, red eyes rolling
from so much wandering and confusion
in the desert before they settled
into a sadness like winter—
all there is.

Long ago I watched birds arc
back and forth over iron tracks
outside a city, and departing that life,
I could not see my hesitation as natural,
the jerking toward change and death
the charm of all that is natural.

This angel needs to flee
his canvas for a damp cave
where the hurt will not be indelible.
As he flutters into the next
day, his eyes will clear
and open fully.

But here, he'll suffer in place
like all who cannot make casual the past.
This morning a seeding of birds across the sky
seemed the same as years ago. It was
winter then, and it is winter now.
How do I get back to the corner
where the child I left with someone
else becomes someone else?

I want what the angel cannot have
as I watch birds full of new hearts
dip over a tangle of tracks. But
these birds do not fly out of the past—
unlike each of those expressions
Crivelli must have pondered
before painting sorrow into an angel's face.

◖ *Full Grown*

Here you come at twenty
with a first full beard.

Once this would have occasioned
lather, a straight razor,

and the song of the strap.
Why is it we think of children

in the eternally feminine?
I was surprised when

your nose lost its pug and lifted
to a presence, your jawbone coming

to its own design. And now there is
this suggestiveness in a beard.

I grew giddy once, then backed off
and frowned at the Bearded Lady

in the midst of moonlit dung—
even then there was a hint

that few will come out of this
the smooth, round child of the mother.

A Short History of Stray Bullets

Three days ago, I tried to save my son
through the mail, saying *quickly, go
back to school, do not so much as go
out of doors.* I could see the yellow
sand dunes arrayed with one more
war for history. I saw him and centuries
of young standing stock still in the distance.
So, I wrote him to head for shelter,
dodge, jump, hop over it; be an agile
body with the feet under rifle fire.

He telephoned to say he'd received my letter
and dreamed of tanks grinding
beneath his window, and what's more,
he had dreamed of me—it was deer season
again, and a woman was in the woods
playing with her dog. Then he heard
the guns and knew he was the son
looking at his mother. He was staring
through binoculars, only his eyes touching
that red blotch on my stomach.

As I drove home on the back road,
a car rode my bumper; lights, ice blue
and spinning, tailed me until I pulled
aside. Then I saw it was a pickup
that swerved wildly, two men laughing,
their heads bobbing before the gun rack
as one stomped it to the floor,
exhaust swirling the air.

This was neither the hunters
nor the tank from my son's dream.
I saw a rifle move by at close range.

On the late news, the commentator's speaking
of *privilege and birth, the luck
of the draw*—why it is that one child
should be taken from his sofa in mid-nap
by an eighteen-bullet spray while
another sleeps among trees and painted houses.
It's a loaded thought,
these accidents of birth.

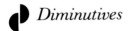 *Diminutives*

Today, it is hours
before you turn into
my daughter, my in-law,
the outlaw my body would not
give up to me. And
here I am wandering
the back roads of Pinellas
to fetch you something wild,
refusing myself
the plots of fenced gardens—
tinted hibiscus,
those spoiled violets
laid out north of the orange tree.
I twist reedy stems
crowned with golds, pinks,
and then your favorite
blue. With Spanish moss
I tie the bridal bow.

Late last night,
your mother brought out
the round happiness
of you at twelve months old—
a photo—saying you looked
just like my son.
I sensed the next sprout of logic,
knowing him as a mirror-me:
the three of us sitting
on a porch,

twined and held together
as if planned to be.

I stood in as you,
walking down the aisle,
your good-luck double
at the rehearsal. Until
a baffled minister
held up his hand,
saying *stop, wait,*
I'm confused. So see,
you almost lost your peacock,
as from that twilit altar
my son smiled and threw
one gold wink at me.

—*for Andrea*

Two Daughters

At length in February,
I wonder why I feel like nobody's
daughter, left with the pulse
of a woman who was always heading
away.
       But today, mother, it's you
who comes back as the one left
homesick from birth, your mother
dead in the influenza of 1918,
leaving you to a Daddy
with a big cigar, who handed you over
to your Granny and headed up east.
Your life
           moved upstream with her to Bella Vista,
where you glued lightning bugs to your ears.
Decked out with stars, you flitted the pitch-
black levee nights and waited for Daddy
to come blow smoke rings, wink at you
and Ida, your Granny
                    who died when you were
twelve, leaving you to her husband, Bough—
no one knows just how he disappeared. He was
the one you would point at in the album,
squinting from under his Panama hat,
leaning on the sugarcane wagon.
Once you read the white ink on the black page
to me: *Handsome Bough, the summer Ida
passed on.* That was the summer you gave up
the lightning bugs
                    and were passed back down

the river to Marguerite, the aunt who thought
life was no place for school. Life
was tall and handsome. Laughing.
And soon she danced you out of school,
over to France, then up to Devon
where I can still hear you telling
of strawberries big as thumbs sucked
down in whipping cream,
of the Englishman who spelled out
he loved you in a bracelet of signal flags
as you danced yourself, careened yourself
into the arms of laughing men.
                                    And here the memories
skip over my thresholds of your nightly
departures until they stop on me at sixteen,
you scoffing at my first love with *too dull,*
so serious. Now, listen to me, I'm your
mother, aren't I?
                        And we stood there staring,
as if this were revelation to us both.

War

My mother said he was real,
not a friend but my father,
home, finished with a war
as he snapped rubber bands
around each lobster's red claws
in that Boston apartment.
Helplessness was what he had
even before the salt poured
its shadowy stream into the kettle;
his lobsters wobbling an altered race
across the linoleum as he winked
and took my mother by the hand,

took me to the bedroom with the foldaway
cot. I sucked my thumb, stroked her satin slip
I kept for the dark, wishing it were dark.
He stood behind her with his big, gold
bourbon glass, his breath moving
into her hair and out of her hair
as he came closer to pull the slip
from my hand, push the thumb from my mouth.
All of Boston's winter rushed the open window,

and he flung the satin slip—in a flutter
it dimmed like a child's ghost
with all that darkness beneath. I saw
the moves of a soldier, his hands
finishing at the window,
seven floors up in the dark.

Unlike a photograph which can be destroyed,
the man carries in his head
a father he would have no part of.
At a railroad crossing
he stops his car to watch
the train cast its light this way
and that, each tree a momentary
comfort, lit like a forest home.

*

Once I asked my father for a picture
of his father, and he looked
through me like cold air
while the night bugs went on thrilling
with late summer. I did not
know that even then
his father, posed in a black vest,
was hidden somewhere in a corner.

*

The next day will arrive and leave
like a blank patch of sunlight
on the cement floor
for the one who refuses
family: leather scrapbook tossed out,
unfilled. A mole pushes the dark
around all day while new fathers
step out into the daylit chores of memory.

*

Hillside kudzu thickens and smells
like hard grape candy: office pockets
of returning fathers. The little son
dances on the car's backseat, waiting
to pick his father's pocket. He can
pick this man out from all those
evening sidewalk marchers. Same corner,
the day after shining like the day before.

*

Monday returns.
How hard men work is a history,
each day passing surely into a flurry
of machinery, ledgers.
Fathers and sons sum each other
up, pacing two strides apart,
then three.
Parting.

*

In the corner of this old desk drawer,
I find a photograph of my father's
forgotten father,
two men with the same eyes.
One harmless now, colorless as leaf mold:
this man he refused to speak of
eyes me with familiar austerity.
Cold—my fathering weather.

*

A man hesitates in a field, reluctant
to go farther than what he knows.
In the starlight he senses something
he never could get to, and murmurs
another September, just what we all need.
His son stares up at him, then out
at the cold distances to the stars,
marks this as memory.

—*for P. L.*

Four

Primer

I had a dream in winter,
sad thoughts with one mountain,
trees,
and two animals.

I walked out on a gray
and white cliff,
not thinking
of those days with you,
until the view turned

treacherous—all that
space
beyond the edge,
fog or smoke rising up.

I needed to touch something,
and suddenly there you were.
There we were with the birds
dropping down a thousand feet
into spring,

that place named for the future.

♩ Free-falling

Outside the coffeehouse a brass quartet
is playing the "Wedding March,"
though neither bride nor groom approaches
on the street. Today everything will be
postponed; it's Friday in a college town,
and no one's thinking in terms
of white. Each high note of exaltation
is sloughed off as some distant
troubadour's outdated posturing.

In the *Collegiate Times* I read
that fifty miles west of here
students are jumping off the bridge
at the New River Gorge. Free-falling,
they call it. Up to a point. These bungee jumpers,
on this first clear day in October, will not
be put off by the body. They'll ride the air
down, testing the strength of forever,
their time between bridge and rapid water.

The coffeehouse empties except for one
student at the next table; head bent,
she holds *The Fine Art of Torture*.
She's trying hard to make it into another's
country. She hears nothing of wedding brass,
and on my oak table I see no hearts
carved, but a swastika sliced in wood.

Outside, the small quartet goes on
sucking in, then blowing out this emptying
October air. It suggests how time spreads
out from sunny acorns to night fires
blazed with oak kindling. Once
I thought the past an amplitude
I could borrow from, then set aside,
like a cold store of history's passions.

 *Rhapsody*

Transport Suitcase. The title
states itself simply for the photograph.
Otto Schwartzkopf stands to the left

with his transport-case of metal,
straps and handle of cardboard.
Rain like a fallen gray veil drapes

Prague while Otto, who seems nine,
probably smiles less after the camera
shutter closes and his fingers continue

their drum on the side of case AAL-351X.
The hat-shop window reflects one old man
standing by Otto, smiling blurrily,

his hand tipping his brimmed hat
to catch the drizzle. Four more metal
suitcases, glinting like wet cutlery,

line the walk by their feet. Neither Otto
nor the old man knows of the holding-town
farther to the east, on the border

between Moravia and Bohemia, where few
care if it's rain or sun glazing the cheek-
bones. They never imagined a storage depot's

enormous wall hung meticulously with one
glossy violin after another,
nailed to the wall without their bows.

From a Vantage Point Overlooking the Battle of Hanging Rock

The soldiers and the horses
need what we all need, more time
to finish making their way
left through my dream.

The whole settlement of a valley
is sliding past my window screen—
horses, wagons, barnyards mixed with soldiers
dressed for the Civil War,

the Battle of Hanging Rock
only a ridge out of reach.
They all appear calm, breezy
as birds in the flyway,

until a white rhinoceros
produces himself with a dusty snort
and settles for my apple tree,
flashing a white grin at a scene

that started amiably enough
with men dressed for shiny-buttoned combat,
mounted on horses, gliding
expertly toward Hanging Rock.

Then, they had my permission,
and they had a time of it in heavy boots,
the horses in an orderly country rampage,
until this valley kingdom

vanished, leaving me
to a rhinoceros staking out
my apple tree—war,
the grinning white hide of a dream.

Rings

One final brute raising,
and the circus heads
for its wintering grounds

where the trapeze lady
will find her windfall self,
the air no longer

such a heady affair as it was
at the top of the tent,
at the height of November.

Florida's warm wind offers
little élan to the tightrope man,
his nets packed ponderously

away, one gold sunup after another
washing in on the coast of flowerland.
And the clown must keep his fingers

out of the gaiety of greasepaint,
his smile blue now, and nothing
more as evening arrives

for the trick horse and dog,
staked, pacing without applause.
Can the ringmaster recover

his rich baritone over warm ale
and billiards? It was his
big top that circled the ordinary

for a season of disguise:
children laughing
at the melancholy clown;

the midget, young again
with room to grow, flaunting
himself as a little one;

the high-wire family
shaping a life of balance
on air while the elephants

lift gray torsos, adding grace
to tonnage. They rise,
sway off slowly on all twos,

leaning heavily on each others'
backs, making it look easy
for buoyant animals

and flying people.

In those first moments of spring
at Ed's place, we spoke of moonlight—
how last night on Highway 64 a moonlit horse
shot out of its pasture and into the man
driving home from a poker game,
his private apocalypse arriving
for the moment when two lives confront
and leave as a single signal.
Who could have imagined such horse-dazzle
at life's end? Ed said it made him think
of horseblinders, the tunnel vision
of a guy who once sat down next to him
in a diner and proceeded to gobble
Ed's 2 A.M. meatball sandwich as if
he did not exist.

         Maybe the moon
was loose that night too, tidying up
a strange imbalance that later
I drive home through—yolky moon
over the mountains, and I am
still imagining that plunging horse
when up ahead on the back road
come three jostling rumps.
Peasant skirts shag the gravel
until four hooves appear on each,
and it's three goats prancing the potholed night.
They do not scatter for my horn
but dare the headlights with silvery coats
and windy goatees, these beasts of revelation
lighting out upon the highway.

 *Daughter*

A herd of cows stare
from the locust grove,
and I recall you saying how at first
that man tried to make fuzzy sense of her
as a deer—some warm, dumb animal
lifted from the highway,
riding his fender toward death—
the possibility of the antlers
being a bike's handlebars as remote
as his beery, midnight world.

You've gone back and back to that
pebbled side of the road,
looking for what you cannot say.
Some reason why it was a daughter
and not a deer veering heavily
onto his fender. To him, just deer
until her hair or arm flashed wildly,
his headlights torching the *she* of it.

Now you are left with an occasional
deer to study for a lifetime
the instant it flees or freezes
in your headlights: beer, deer,
beer—shadows of you are around me
as through the locust trees
cow eyes bloom like all
the dark matter that peers,
then disappears in space.

—*for Barri*

Take it back to the hills
where no distance was too great.
There was little speculation
as the earth parted from the sky,
and the stars had no need
to be arranged or touched.

The desert lay forever
strung with networks of date palm,
and the Southern Cross lit sands
streaming through the scheme of things.
Its light was enough
to etch the landscape with design.

It was enough to have the trees,
winter ridges crawling with them
into the twilight. The heavy ewe
slept in the herd, never dreaming
of barns, a future of holding-rooms.
The wind had not called for an altar
to blow on, candles for proof.

 *Prediction*

Lightning rods rise in accusation above
firehouses and the American Red Cross

while the town's one doctor
surrounds himself with hypodermics,

suspecting disaster in his own,
small way. He's heard tales

of cyclones lifting the outskirts
of Bombay and fires that peel back

lives on the Serengeti Plain. There
are no funerals on the plains, only cattle

skulls that flare and vanish
like towns on the desert edge.

Shame

This little ostrich takes it in the neck
from three drunk college boys.
Out to prove themselves,
fueled, aroused to scale
the fence of the Animal Research Lab,
they want to choke the life,
to take the life, and feel the air
leave one elegant, long windpipe.
All six hands, their thirty fingers
grapple to squeeze the thrusting
blue skin. They want to hear
their own grunts,
then squawks of the wild-eyed fowl.
Eyes bald and bulging,
they dance the cage at the throat

of one tall, crumpling bird.

*

And this little moose loses it
to the grown-ups
near the salmon-sparkled Mirimishi.
She took it in the brain,
plugged, brought down into that old,
sorry animal heap.
Each of the hunters,
one daring the next,
unzippers to fuck and bear his flesh-
hard tool down into fresh kill,
the warm, sexual pouch.

The rest of the kingdom sniff,
back off.
For a while.
At least for these moments
while men lean into what's changing
to carcass, the sun setting,

earth rolling over into night.

Five

Terrestrial

Imagine this green
planet moving steadily

through space,

macaws clutching
wet banana leaves,
and elephants planted
firmly on earth as it spins.

Speechless, the animals
beat across the wild plains,
never taking stock

of balance or reflection
peering back from the drinking hole.

◗ *October Bestiary*

Shucks flit the horizon,
then fall earthward

where everything is on the move
this late October day,

crows circling their black fleet
off past the cut cornfield.

Squirrels scamper, the hesitant ones
bled into the highway by cars,

those steady weapons, so unlike
the zigzagging pursuits

of the morning dog
who cornered a snapping turtle

on his way from ditch to pond.
Big turtle caked with bulrushes,

the stench of time, his thick neck
and claws older than any

Moses in the marsh.
Even the fish are headed somewhere,

the suicidal carp at it again,
our neighbor yelling *that fish*

is jumping up and out of your pond.
It's a strange time, this space

of ambulatory fall fever. Yesterday
a fawn followed a child out of the field

to play house pet, sleeping on the sofa,
eating packs of Lucky Strike,

the rest of the animal world intent
on dispersal. I focus binoculars

on bear cubs stumbling off
with their mother toward high country;

four wild turkeys strut
their feathered stuff

while a buck nods antlers
as if in assent. By sundown

flies darken the screen door,
join this frail racket of abundance.

Think about It

The ground's a stew of apple-rot,
white meat opening for bees
to stick their faces to.

Sometimes eyes stick out from fields—
the wolfish dog's one ice blue eye
like chicory at noon, and up the road

a hunter's camouflage glove blows
from one place to the next,
never fitting in. This is the October

I can imagine arriving without me
in it. When I look up from reading,
the field's a blur of crows, my eyes

blurring to all but the print
about primroses on page 53:
they are lucidly yellow in old fields

and waste places. So there are places
as wasted as this valley when it's adrift
in fog and voices herding cattle call out,

unseen—words meaning only the world's
a cold well, the bluish thunk of apples
dying onto ground. Winter is almost here,

I can feel it happening and want
the cat to be my good omen as she rolls
on concrete in the sun. An old sundial,

my mind ranges to a time of heat
and loss. Suddenly I am lost again
with my mother at the end of a car line

in Havana, castanets and palm fronds
clicking as we walk, not a coin
jangling in her purse. Listen,

why not stop all of this?
Stop. Think about it
or not, the mind will go on

changing like apples
in the sun, like crows
circling the field.

Bedside Story

It was a circular love
that woke me, brought me
upright one night
when she decided to end it again
with a note. I knew
and moved more surely than ever
down the hallway toward her bed
as if I were her ghost arriving,
and not her child. There was
this arrangement: her eyes
closed, the lamp burning
above a bottle and a note.
I saw the words flaring
to a point, to the silent
core of a note loaded to hold me.

Santa Rosa Island

Nights, the moon would come
clay red from the gulf
as she drifted from window to window

insisting it was the moon
that stole her sleep.
But she'd lost him.

He left her once, twice,
until all that remained
of her Navy man was an outline—

a beach, water and waves.
She kept handing me photographs
of waves, raising and lowering him

on the deck of his ship.
In the tides she heard
a homecoming, steady, steadfast

as make-believe. Return. And return.
He would not come back.
So the dunes became a map to somewhere

her feet could not get enough of,
a lap she kept to climb into,
homesick as any child.

Wanting It

At night my long-dead and slow-
dissolving mother swam back.
There she was again in her element,
the gulf, high white dunes sloping behind.
Changed, she was happy
as I had always wanted her to be.
In a newly watered voice
she declared that I was to take note,
finally she'd moved her life to the sea.
She dove and curled in the surface waters,
pleased as any creature to be faced
with all that green. She was smiling
at what life had never been,
something of the dolphin mouth
apparent in her nature.

I pack carefully
the green suitcase from my first
marriage, twenty-seven years ago.
I lay out black to be the soft-spoken,
new-and-improved mother of the groom.
To take my dead mother along,
I put on her wedding gift,
the Black-Starr watch
my father inscribed with *Tink*
and *April, 1939.* Then
I drop her lapis locket
into a side pocket, the way she
dropped into the dark years ago.

As the plane takes off,
I feel pressure of the sucked-back life.
Like an old photograph growing lush
with color, I fill in
the bride decades old in me,
the April girl in my mother
turning white veiled
so many springs from here—
all of us brides dispatched
and squeezed in tight.

The woman across the aisle,
already into the next phase,
reads *Natural Childbirth:*
Select a Focal Point.
I choose you, my son

for whom I'm carrying
a spectral gift: the grandmother
you barely knew.

At this elevation, we must appear
romantic, night-lights adrift
in the clouds, an airlift
of star embryos headed
toward your wedding—
watches, dates, lockets,
the young bride and dead mother
harboring in me.
The stakes are kaleidoscopic.

The stewardess, balancing
vodka and lemons,
gives a half-smile.
Then a big grin,
holding a finger to the air.
She's turning, changing.
Her hands fatten, pinken, and grow small.
And I am seeing you,
the groom, only minutes
into your years:
how soft and irretrievable
each of your fingers is.
The wedding veil shifts and magnifies.

Secrets about Nothing

I saw it first as suggestion,
words held on the tongue
when our reflected faces,
lit by lightning,
flashed in the window glass,
then disappeared. We both
drew in our breaths
and looked away.

It echoes in the stillness after
words, the narrative
welling up in your eyes—
like a hollowness that follows
the hunting dog after he raises his eyes,
then voice to the yellow moon.

And it magnifies in the eyes
of those no longer young
as they take on heavy faces—
the slow, puckering
thread of age
stitching loosely across the mirror.

Once it hung in a crystal charm,
this secret about nothing,
and at its center
my children's faces turned
to old men's,
and old men's back to boys'.
I play checkers, crowning nothing.

That year you said it would be
a cold spring, with no grass
or petals. We sentenced ourselves
to the conditional, and I began
sucking on air
thinning to sweetness at the core.

Tonight the eaves fill with wind,
lightning whitens us,
our bed. By the window screen
a book blows open
to one blank page, then another.
Passion begins here.

In Spite of Forgetting

After the war, I wished
one steeple would reappear like spiraling
volition, and then to have its chimes

                              sway out once
more after the dismembering explosions
I was warned of from a sick bay—
that voice saying *never let this happen*
to you.

           *

But the snow-hushed woods bear a directive.
Forget.
        Make it an epoch caught in crossfire,

                         then erasure.
Nail blame to a particular person, a place.
Say the scuffle ends at a village edge,
and that the blame rests with one of the two
figures standing there, reaching out.
                   See
how quickly the faulty one's hands
                     become logical
and appear to sign for *therefore*
               and *for this reason,*
forgetting the shots fired in the square.

           *

Or perhaps the memory begins with guns
at a border crossing.
          In the tropics, anthills
nightly balloon three feet high,

and each day small black bodies are torched.
Afternoons, the oleander
                    takes on lush distance
in the rains, high above the body counts.
Sweet scent above the bodies.
This is a landscape to be studied, in relief.

                    *

Sometimes the forgetting descends at dusk,
that widow light
                    when the footsteps fade,
when grass embankments and hillside
animal paths lose their geography
of war: field grave
                    or the dead's route
                    down to the sea.

                    *

In such a twilight I suspect
it's summer in a calmed place
until I hear
                    across the water
a rifle repeat
as a figure makes an overarching gesture
to rise, and keep rising,
before it sinks down through the air again.

                    *

One death can be an outline,
black-edged calling card

              floated to the surface.
The weather should be mild and clear for burial
at sea
      I knew one once who had it that way,
and afterwards there were no markers
or the creak of metal rigging.

           *

Look at this pond. See how the trout's splash
eliminates the perfectly
               reflected moon.
And before, I was gazing at an underwater
expanse of grasses
           swaying like spires
far below in Warsaw or Harlan County,
steeples under black smoke,
              under water
                   in another time.

The Springhouse

sits astride this spongy hole in the planet.
Sycamores whiten at dusk, fruit bats

home in around the pond, and there's one
visitor that didn't make it in

for a drink: raccoon at rest by the spring-
house, his scurry now settled into

carcass, while the stove in the brambles
sprouts a welcome of newly warmed forsythia.

An unlaced work shoe, half-full of water,
leads me to look at my own bare feet,

damp with spring fever, the grass scattered
with feathers the mallard left, each quill

once a jade slash in white weather.
Tonight, new moon rising, this village

storefront holds sway as I pry open the door
on a dark wishing-room of water.

Under these eaves, it will be afternoon
in a temperate zone all summer.

A Shared Life

The horses nuzzle,
and bluebirds scatter from the fence post
like Sunday's children at a picnic.
But who promised all would be this idyllic

                      with the fences up
or down—the black dog shot today, bleeding
among the farmer's dead pheasants, the brown dog
uncontrollable in his pursuit of cows,
cows bemoaning the fenced life
the dog charges through.

Even the dozing cattle settle
under a tree house

                not made by children.
Platform nailed high in a field oak,
where at night deer arrive with eyes

                      like porch lamps snapped on
                      in the mist
as flashlight and double-barreled shotgun

                        plug each in turn,
                        mindless
of the limits.

And there is no end to limits: no end
                to how the guinea hens can't
                fly high enough, to how the pheasants
                can't run far enough, to how the black
                dog ran straight for the pheasants
                and now is laid out in a patch

of bronze feathers, while cows
flee the brown dog, flee
in four directions like the simpleminded
or an early fall wind, the animal warden
speeding across the beeline of 311 North
to say he don't want to cause nobody
no heartbreak, but those two dogs
broke the law; and behind him by noon
comes the woman in the gray sedan,
taking a skiddy turn up to the dead
dog's porch to yell that the radio's so loud
it's spooking her cows. Oh, woe

unto all these dismal marriages in the fields,
woe to those with the vacant
                              or intelligent brown eyes,
to those with talons, canines, or cuds.

Even on calm days, cows press their hides
to the barbed wire
                    like noses to the window——
                    a wish, perhaps, to be one of the lost,
to be one of those with secret paths in sunlight,
hidden compasses for midnight.
A wish not to be
                  one of these cows who rush
                  each dawn ahead of this dervish of a dog,
                  every breath a puffed remnant

of those lost to the fog a year at a time—
our animal universe tail to mouth,
tumbling into a rosy, beastly oblivion.

The Iowa Poetry Prize Winners

1 9 8 7

Elton Glaser, *Tropical Depressions*
Michael Pettit, *Cardinal Points*

1 9 8 8

Bill Knott, *Outremer*
Mary Ruefle, *The Adamant*

1 9 8 9

Conrad Hilberry, *Sorting the Smoke*
Terese Svoboda, *Laughing Africa*

The Edwin Ford Piper Poetry Award Winners

1 9 9 0

Philip Dacey, *Night Shift at the Crucifix Factory*
Lynda Hull, *Star Ledger*

1 9 9 1

Greg Pape, *Sunflower Facing the Sun*
Walter Pavlich, *Running near the End of the World*

1 9 9 2

Lola Haskins, *Hunger*
Katherine Soniat, *A Shared Life*